SIMPLE GRAPH ART

by: Erling and Dolores Freeberg

D0550401

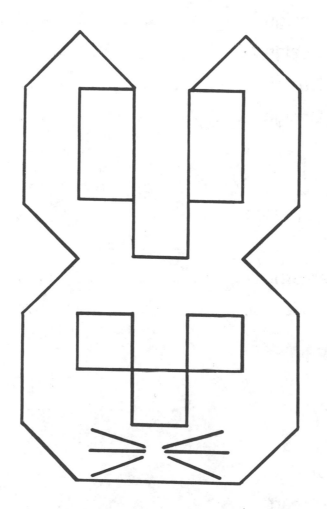

Teacher Created Materials, Inc.
P.O. Box 1040
Huntington Beach, CA 92647
©1987 Teacher Created Materials, Inc.
Made in U.S.A.

ISBN 1-55734-095-1

TABLE OF CONTENTS
(Listed in order of difficulty)

MYSTERY PICTURE DIRECTIONS

This graph art activity book is a compilation of kindergarten-first grade level pictures which are designed to fit graph paper squares. The child colors in the squares on graph paper according to directions on a direction sheet and a mystery picture appears.

OBJECTIVES

1. beginning reading skills (left-right, top-bottom sequence)
2. beginning graphing skills
3. transference
4. small motor coordination
5. following specific directions
6. concentration on a task
7. paying attention to details

DIRECTIONS

1. Reproduce a blank graph sheet and a mystery picture directions sheet for each child.
2. The child should *not* see the answer key picture prior to doing the activity.
3. The teacher should demonstrate to the class how to follow the directions and should provide opportunity for practicing first. The first four designs in this book are meant to help the child learn how to do this activity.

    SAMPLE: ROW 1 - Color 6 [B] 1 [O/R] 1 [R/O] means;
    In row 1 color the first six squares blue; divide the next square ◻ and color the bottom triangle red and color the top triangle orange according to the color key. Do the same to the next square ◺.

4. The child should cross out each direction as it is completed, and should fold back or cover each row on the directions sheet as it is completed.
5. Any additional features shown in the answer key picture should be added to the completed design, e.g. add eyes, nose, whiskers.

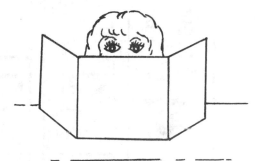

HELPFUL TEACHING HINTS:

1. This activity can be done independently with a higher ability level group *or* it can be done with young children as a group activity under the direct guidance of the teacher and handled as a week-long project (one or two rows a day). Independence comes with practice.
2. Extra graph sheets should be available, because errors might be made on first attempts.
3. Each child's paper should be hidden from others' view while working so that another child will not see the picture before he figures it out himself.
4. The designs having white as one of their colors should be reproduced on manila colored paper so the white will show.
5. The colored finished product will be most attractive if:
    a. the child colors solidly with crayons or marking pens and stays in the lines
    b. the child does *not* outline the squares
    c. the child blends together squares of the same color

COLOR KEY:

R = Red	Y = Yellow	B = Blue	PL = Purple	BK = Black
PK = Pink	G = Green	LB = Light Blue	BR = Brown	GY = Gray
O = Orange	LG = Light Green	T = Tan	W = White	

Mystery Picture #1

		Color Key	R = red O = orange	Y = yellow G = green
1	Color 3	R ₃ Y ₃ O		
2	Color 3	R ₃ Y ₃ O		
3	Color 1	G ₃ R ₃ Y ₂ O		
4	Color 1	G ₃ R ₃ Y ₂ O		
5	Color 2	G ₃ R ₃ Y ₁ O		
6	Color 2	G ₃ R ₃ Y ₁ O		
7	Color 3	G ₃ R ₃ Y		

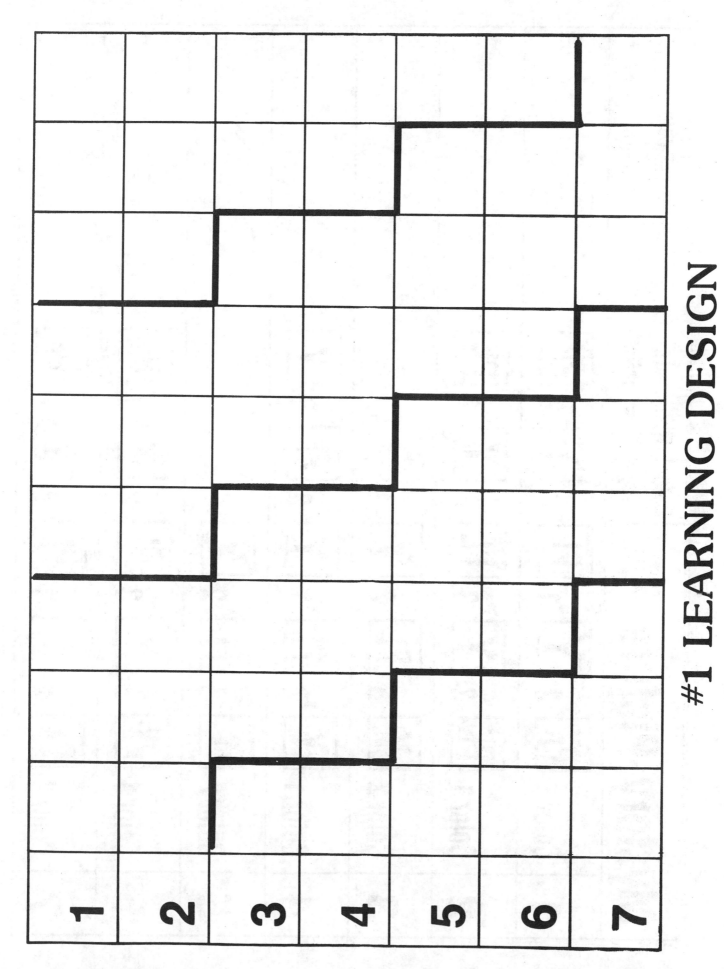

#1 LEARNING DESIGN

5

Mystery Picture #2

Color Key

PK = pink
Y = yellow
PL = purple

#										
1	Color 2	PK	2	Y	1	PL	2	Y	2	PK
2	Color 1	PK	2	Y	3	PL	2	Y	1	PK
3	Color 2	Y	5	PL	2					
4	Color 1	Y	3	PL	1	Y	3	PL	1	Y
5	Color 2	Y	5	PL	2	Y				
6	Color 1	PK	2	Y	2	PL	3	Y	1	PK
7	Color 2	PK	2	Y	1	PL	2	Y	2	PK

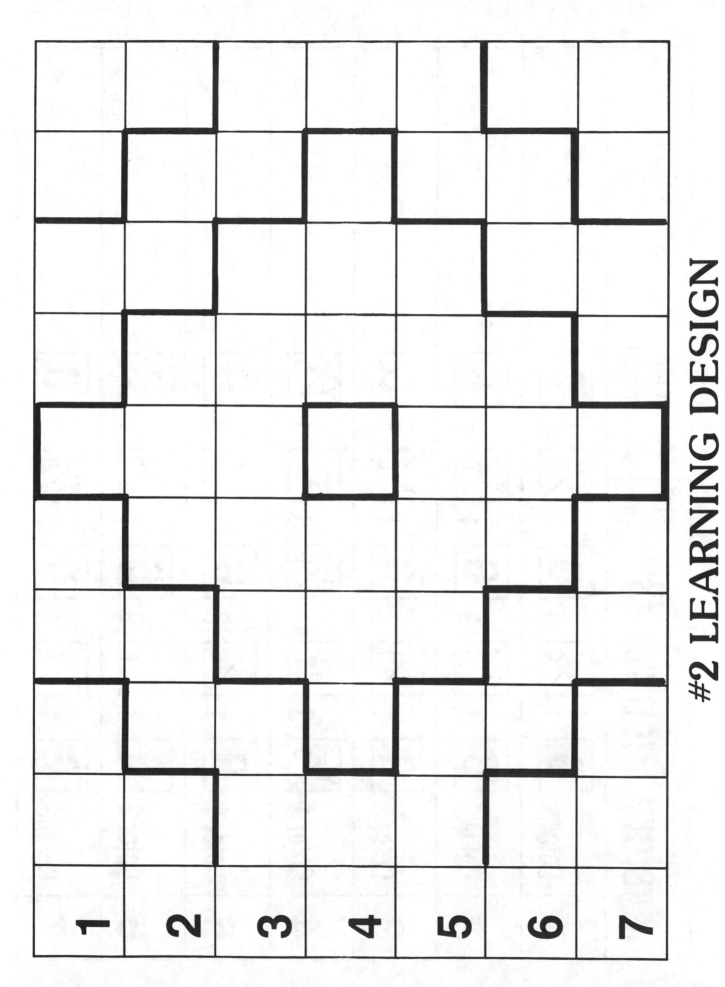

#2 LEARNING DESIGN

Mystery Picture #3

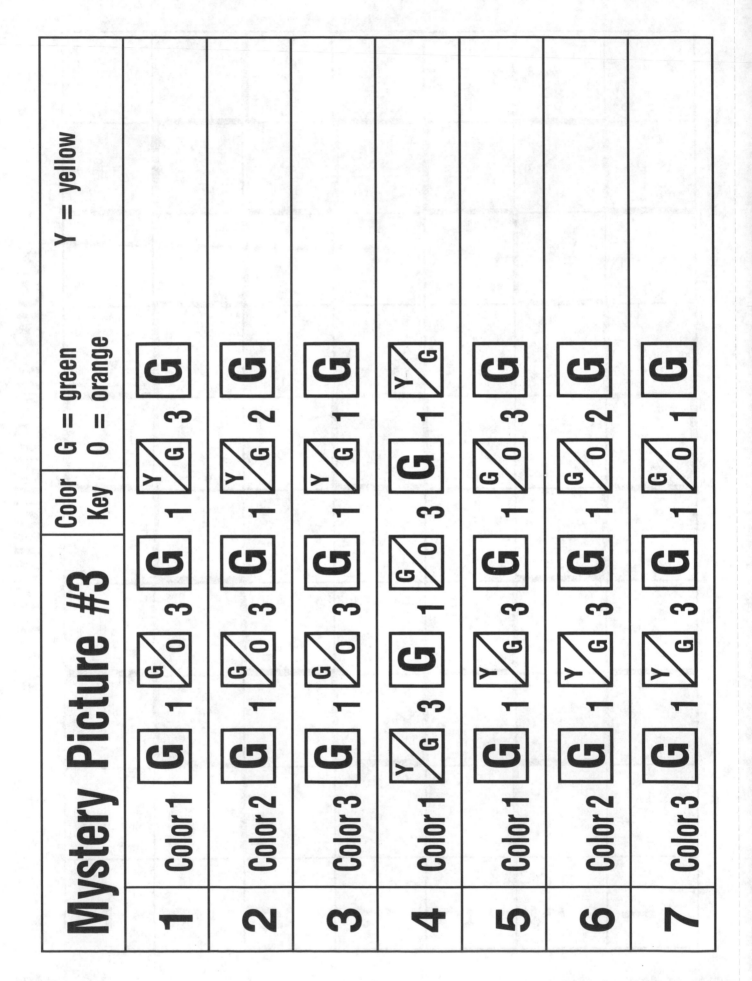

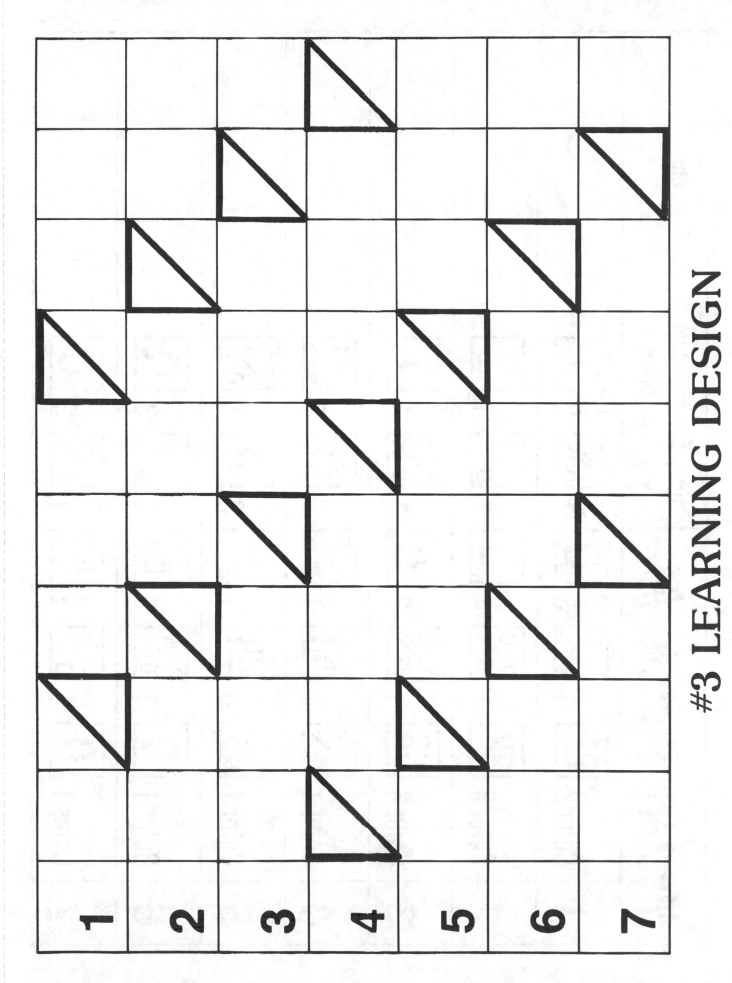

#3 LEARNING DESIGN

#095 Simple Graph Art

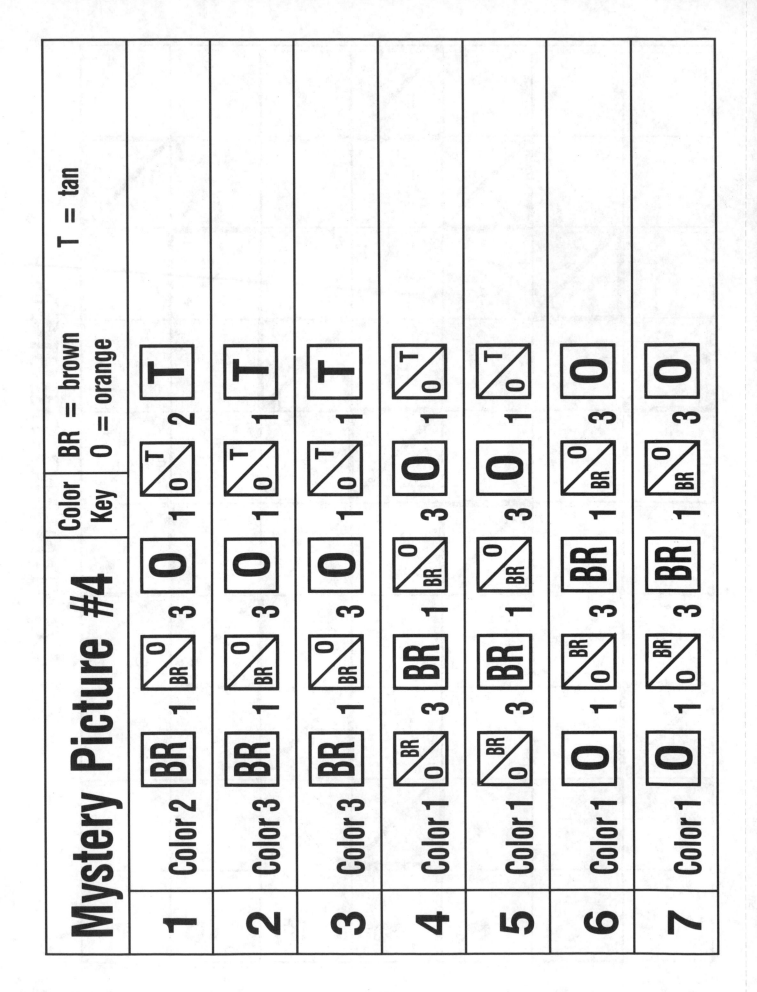

Mystery Picture #4

Color Key: BR = brown, O = orange, T = tan

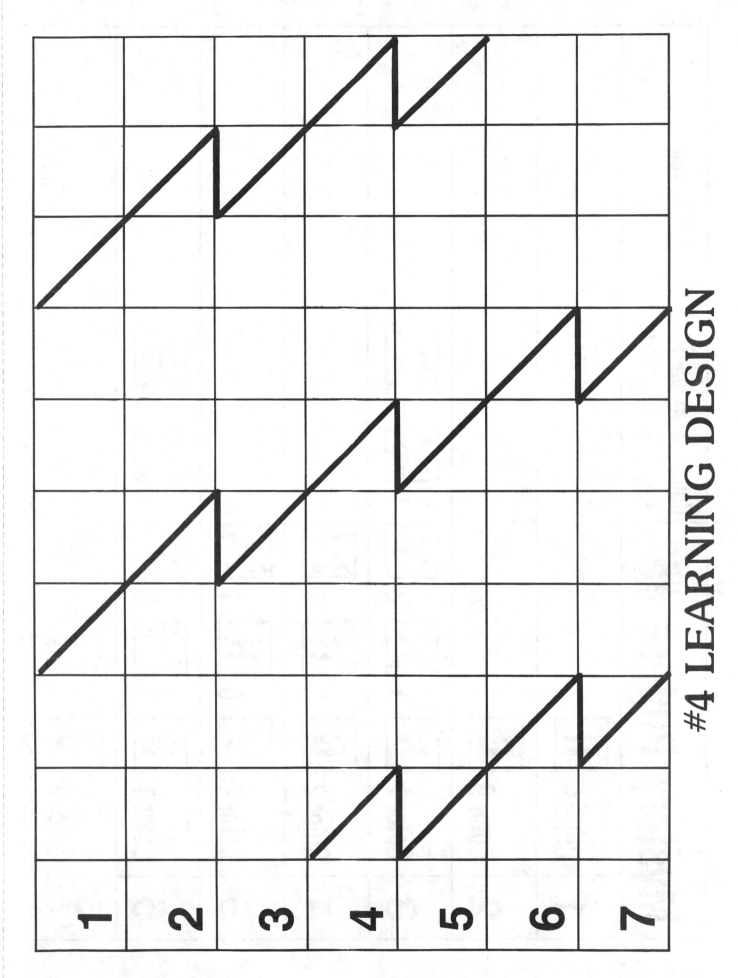

#4 LEARNING DESIGN

Mystery Picture #5

Color Key
B = blue
Y = yellow
R = red

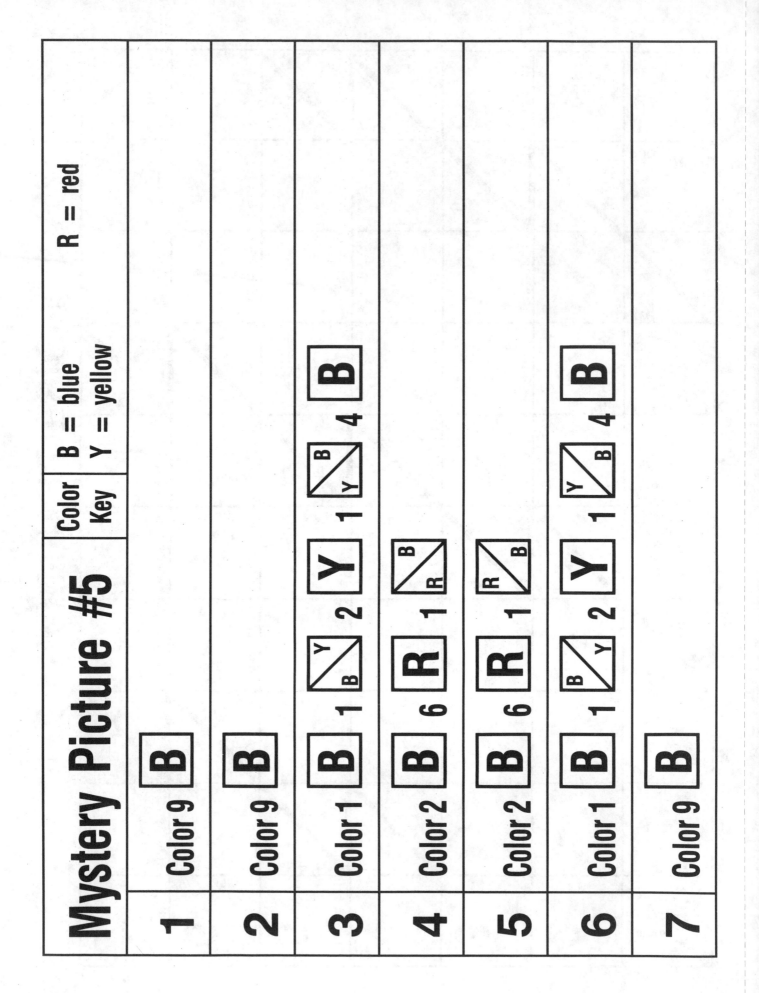

1 Color 9 **B**

2 Color 9 **B**

3 Color 1 **B** | 1 **Y/B** | 2 **Y** | 1 **B/Y** | 4 **B**

4 Color 2 **B** | 6 **R** | 1 **R/B**

5 Color 2 **B** | 6 **R** | 1 **R/B**

6 Color 1 **B** | 1 **B/Y** | 2 **Y** | 1 **Y/B** | 4 **B**

7 Color 9 **B**

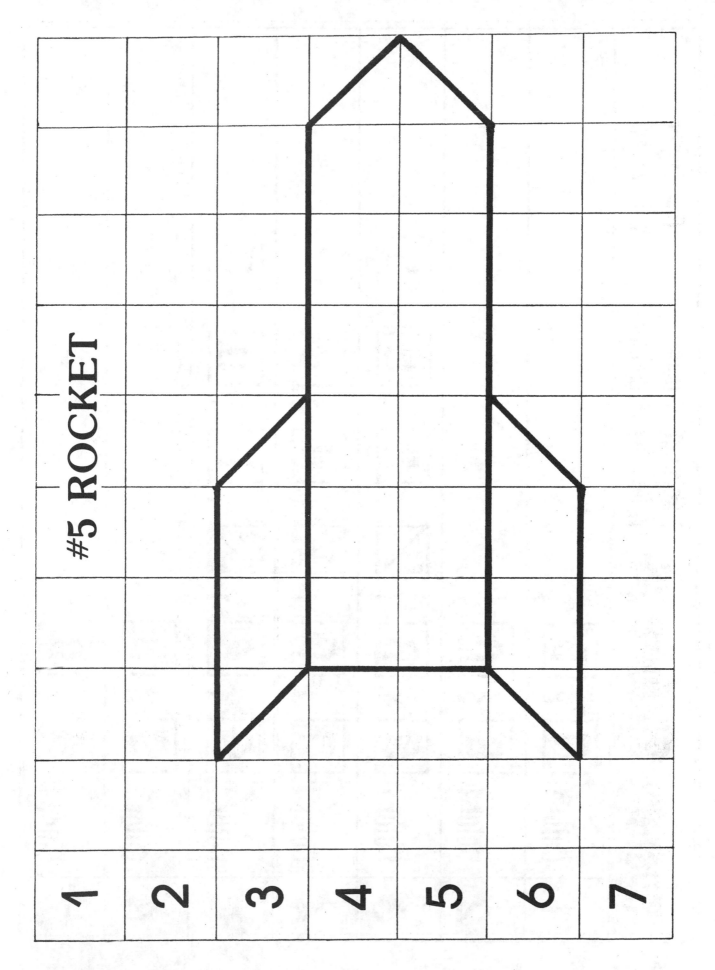

#5 ROCKET

1 2 3 4 5 6 7

Mystery Picture #6

#095 Simple Graph Art

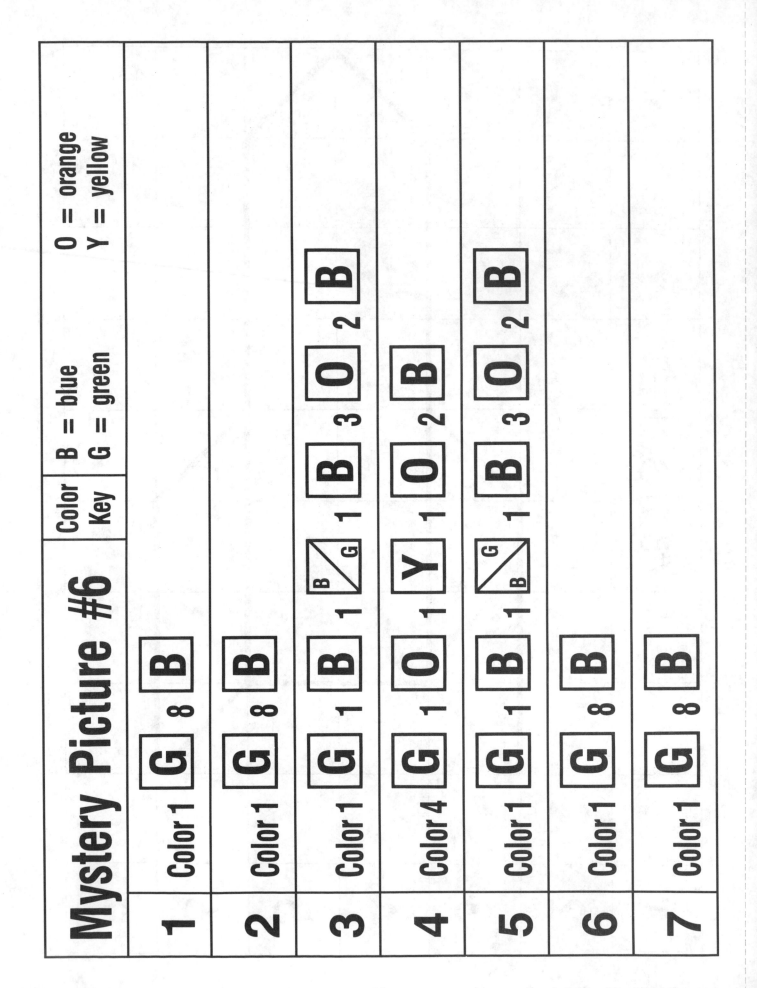

Color Key: B = blue   O = orange
G = green   Y = yellow

1	Color 1	G	8	B						
2	Color 1	G	8	B						
3	Color 1	G	1	B/G	1	B	3	O	2	B
4	Color 4	G	1	O	1	Y	1	O	2	B
5	Color 1	G	1	B/G	1	B	3	O	2	B
6	Color 1	G	8	B						
7	Color 1	G	8	B						

#6 FLOWER

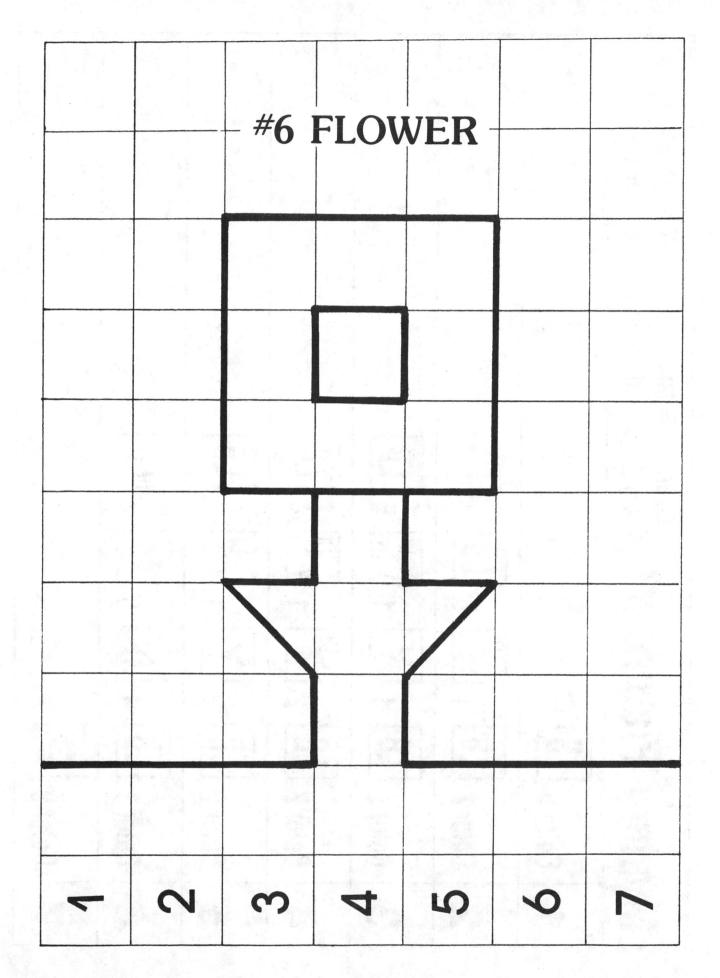

#095 Simple Graph Art

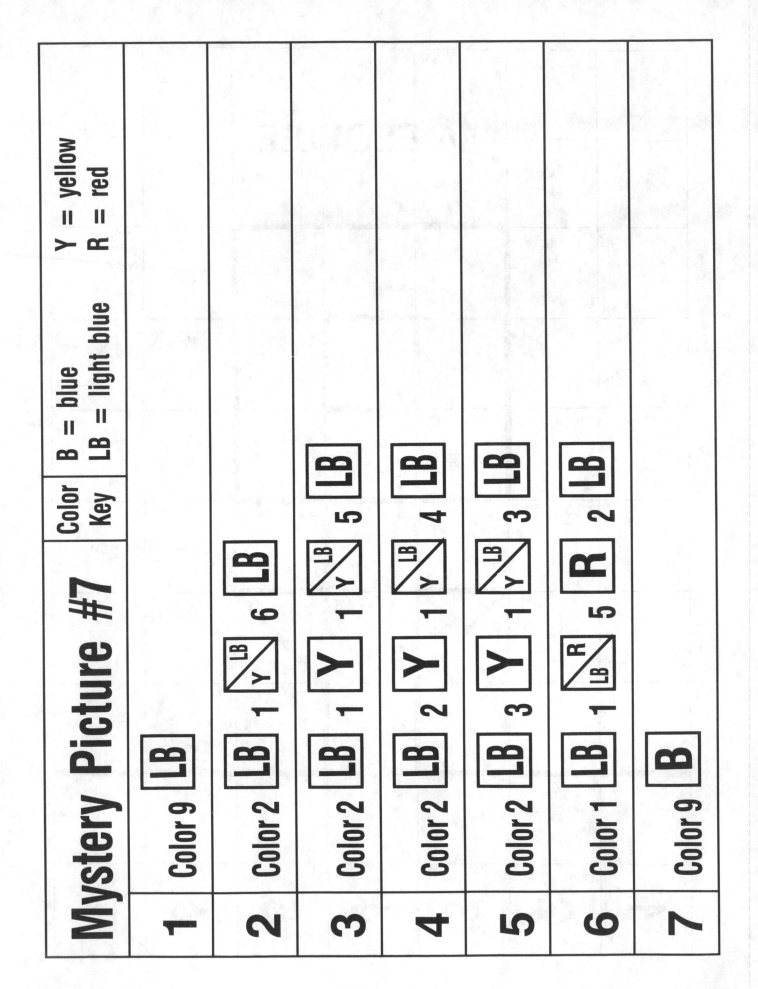

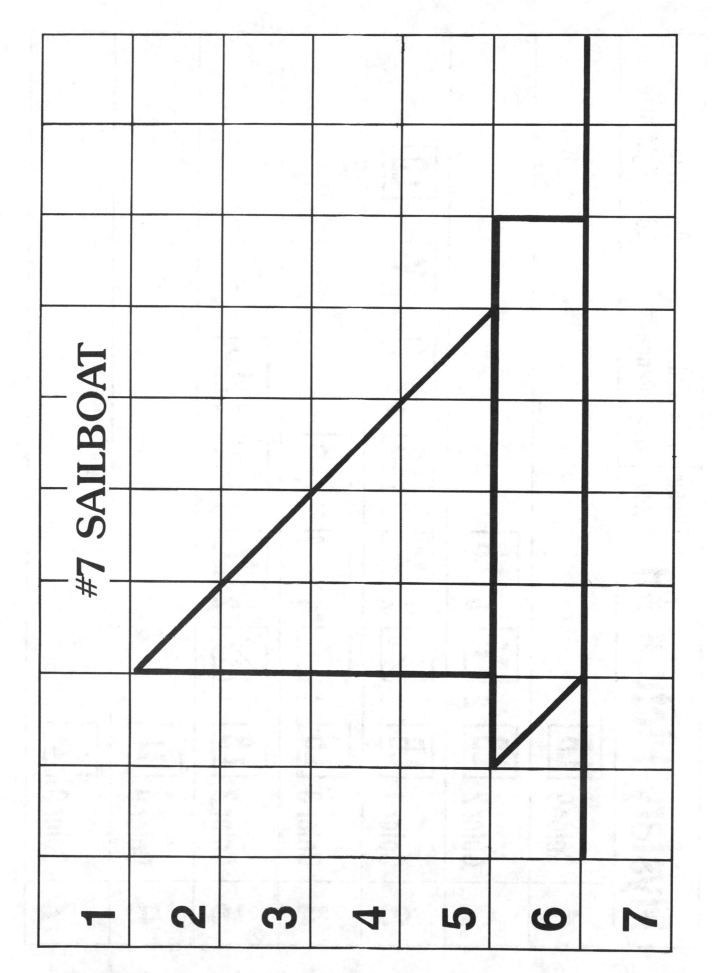

#7 SAILBOAT

1 2 3 4 5 6 7

Mystery Picture #8

Color Key

Y = yellow   B = blue
O = orange   LB = light blue

1 Color 9 [LB]

2 Color 2 [LB] 2 [Y] 5 [LB]

3 Color 1 [LB/O] 2 [Y] 2 [LB] 1 [LB/Y] 1 [Y] 1 [LB]

4 Color 4 [LB] 1 [Y] 1 [Y/LB] 1 [LB]

5 Color 1 [LB] 2 [Y] 1 [Y/LB] 2 [LB]

6 Color 9 [B]

7 Color 9 [B]

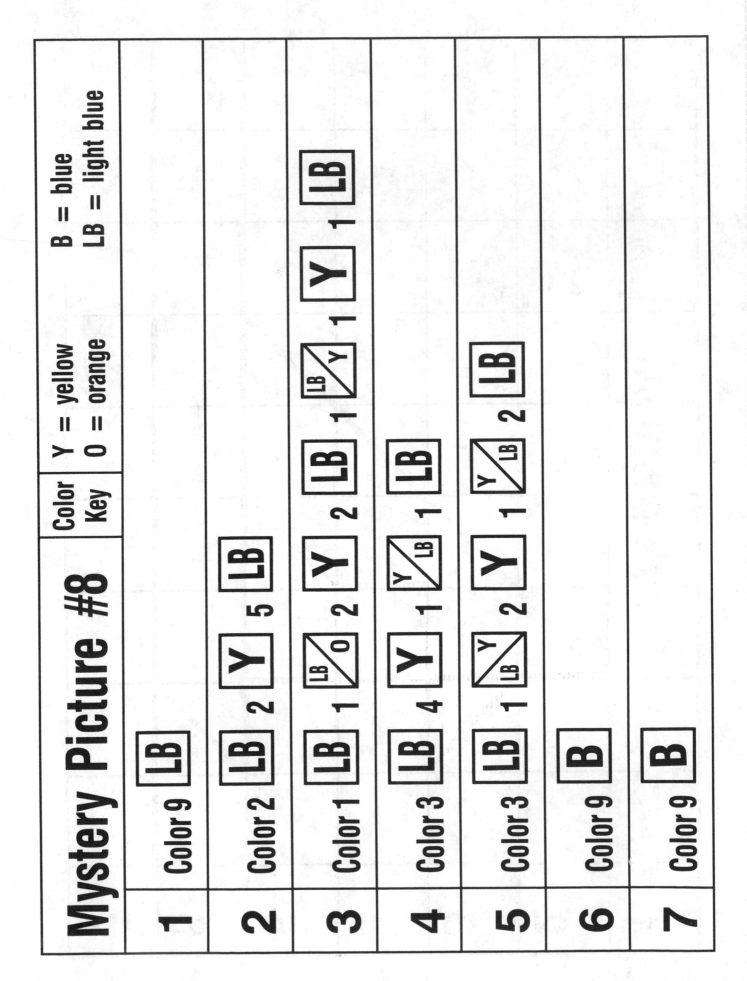

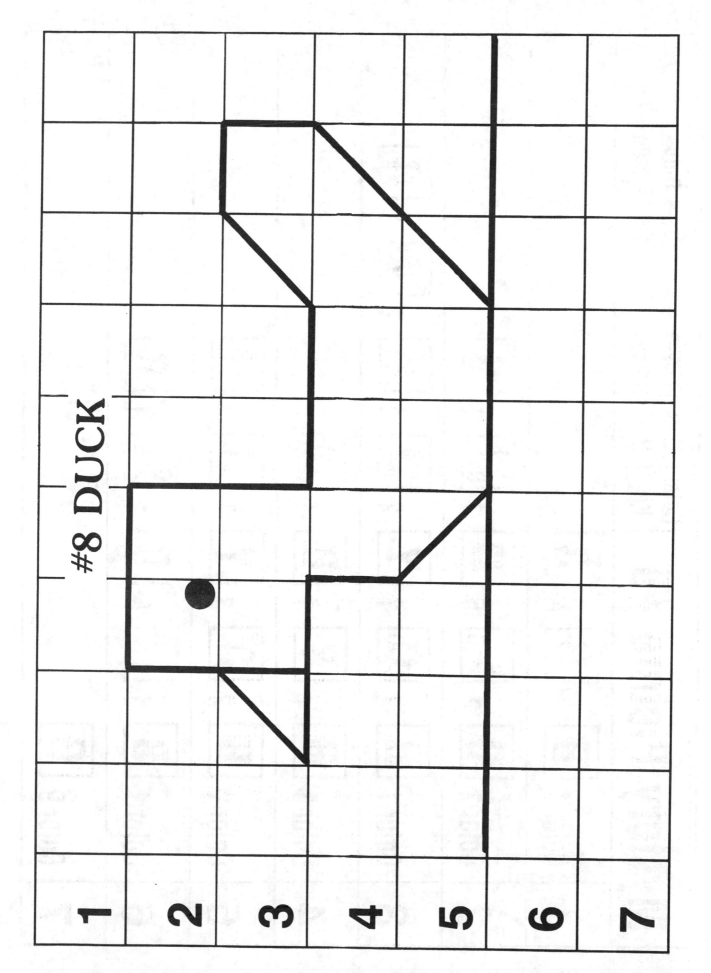

#8 DUCK

#095 Simple Graph Art

Mystery Picture #9

Color Key

O = orange	B = blue
Y = yellow	G = green

1	Color 4 [B] 1 [G] 4 [B]
2	Color 1 [B] 1 [B/O] 5 [O] 1 [O/B] 1 [B]
3	Color 1 [B] 2 [O] 1 [Y] 1 [O] 1 [Y] 2 [O] 1 [B]
4	Color 1 [B] 7 [O] 1 [B]
5	Color 1 [B] 2 [O] 3 [Y] 2 [O] 1 [B]
6	Color 1 [B] 1 [O/B] 5 [O] 1 [O/B] 1 [B]
7	Color 9 [G]

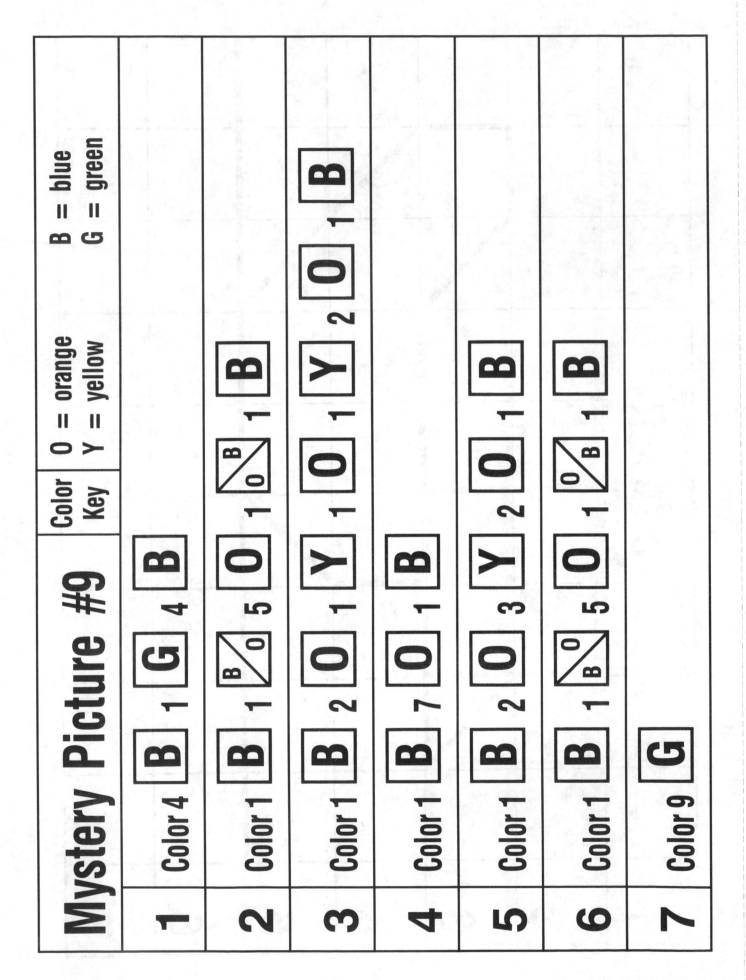

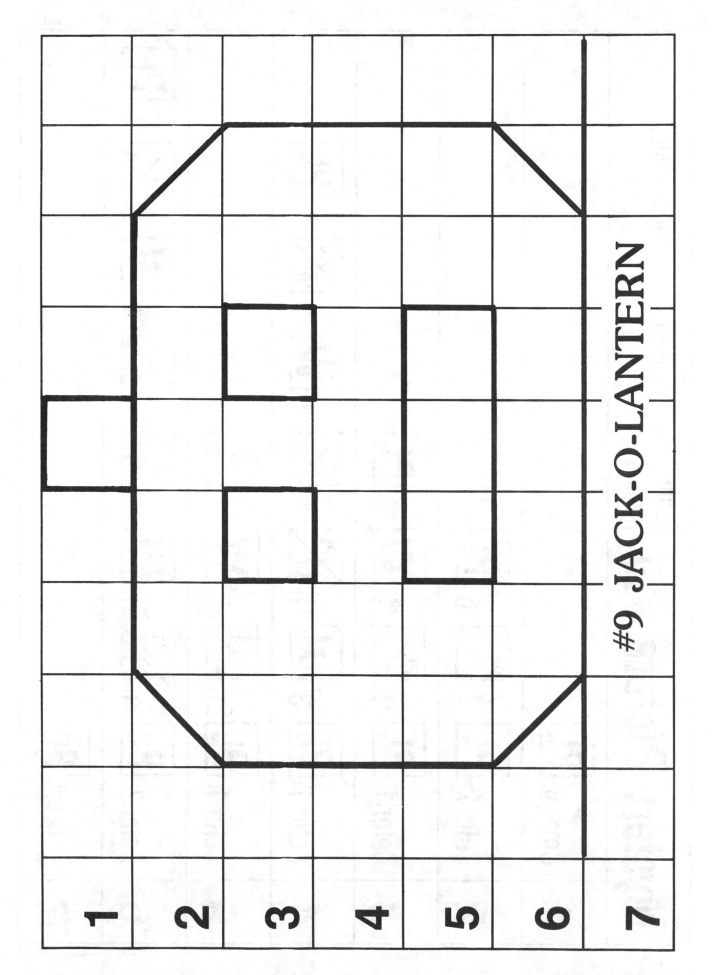

#9 JACK-O-LANTERN

Mystery Picture #10

	Color Key	PL = purple	W = white

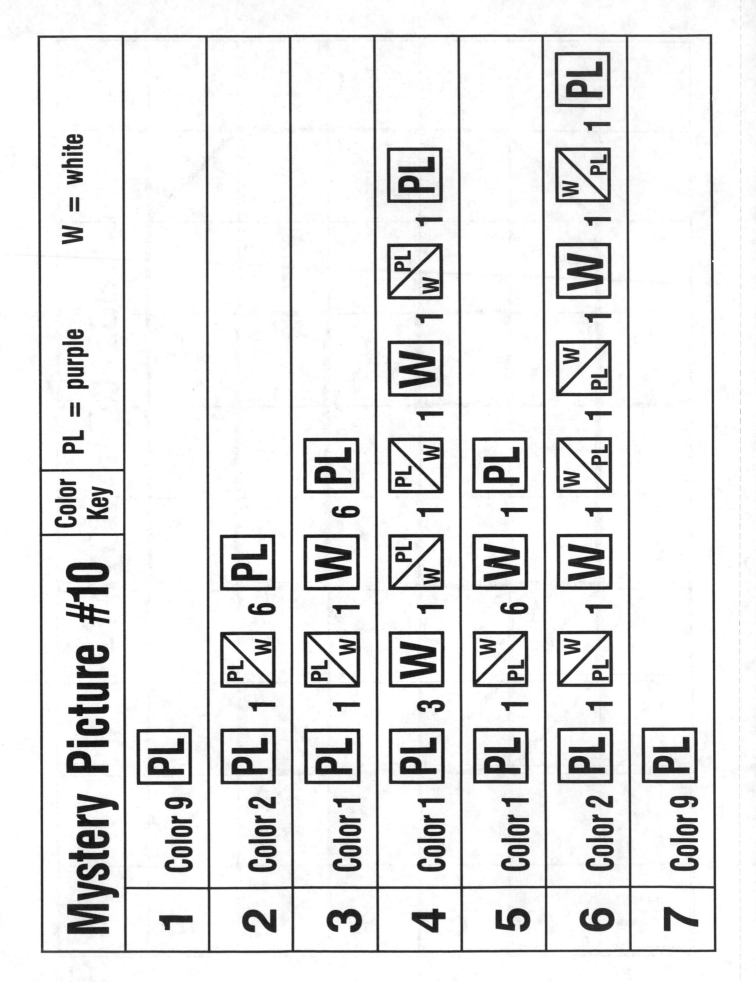

1 Color 9 PL

2 Color 2 PL 1 PL/W 6 PL

3 Color 1 PL 1 PL/W 1 W 6 PL

4 Color 1 PL 3 W 1 W 1 PL/W 1 W 1 PL/W 1 PL

5 Color 1 PL 1 W/PL 6 W 1 PL

6 Color 2 PL 1 W/PL 1 W 1 W/PL 1 W 1 W/PL 1 PL

7 Color 9 PL

#10 GHOST

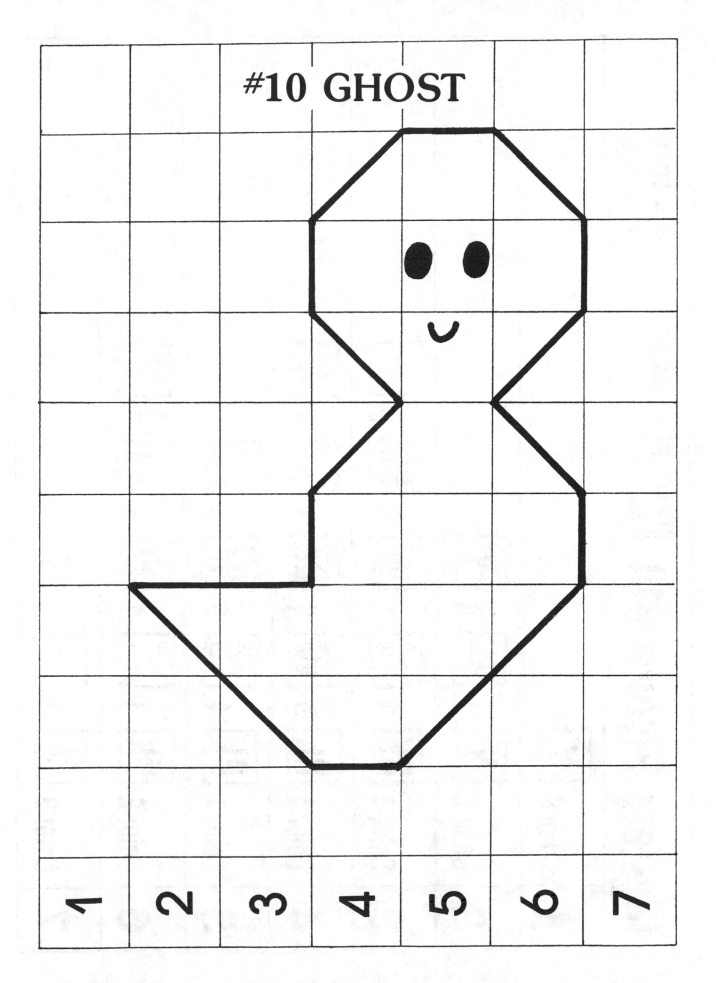

#095 Simple Graph Art

Mystery Picture #11

Color Key
BK = black   O = orange
Y = yellow   LG = light green

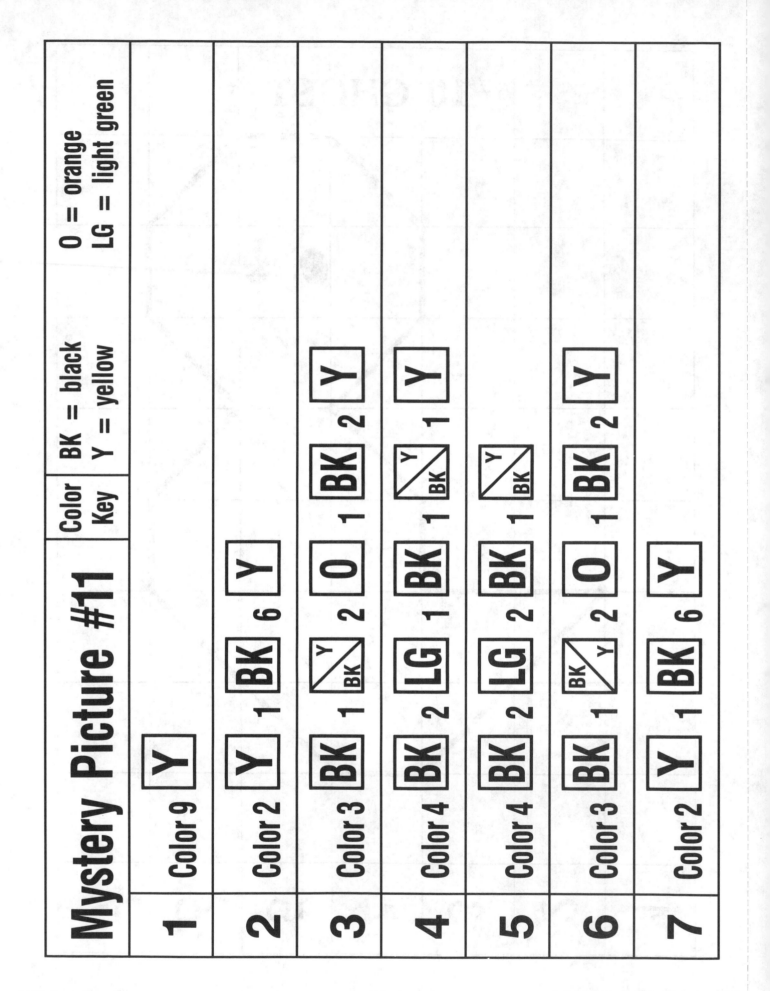

1. Color 9 — Y
2. Color 2 — Y 1 BK 6 Y
3. Color 3 — BK 1 Y/BK 2 O 1 BK 2 Y
4. Color 4 — BK 2 LG 1 BK 1 Y/BK 1 Y
5. Color 4 — BK 2 LG 1 BK 1 BK/Y
6. Color 3 — BK 1 BK/Y 2 O 1 BK 2 Y
7. Color 2 — Y 1 BK 6 Y

#11 WITCH

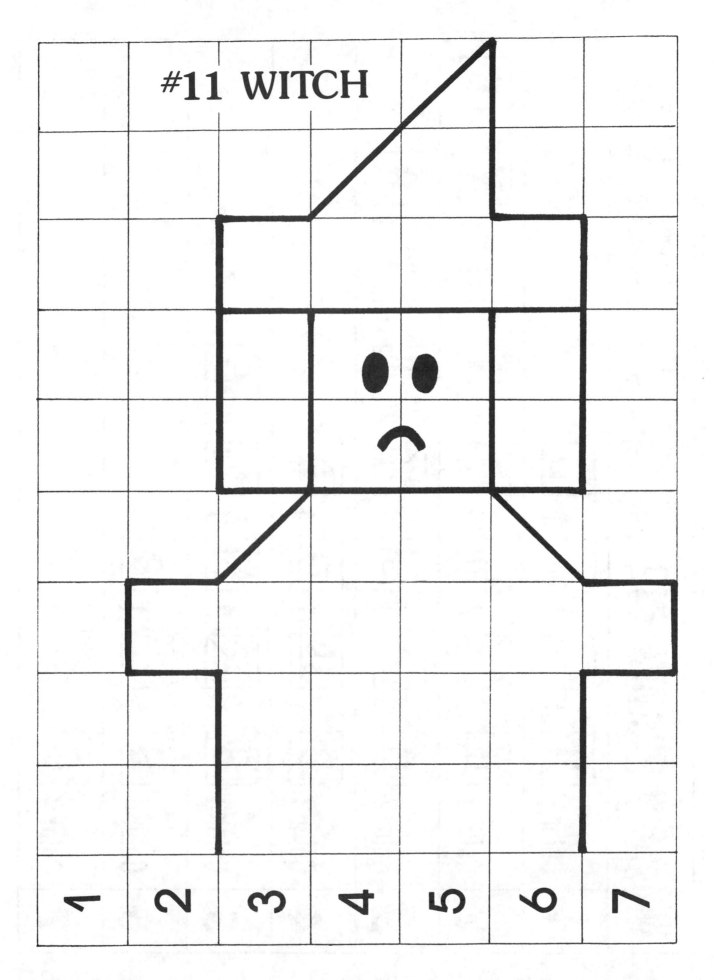

Mystery Picture #12

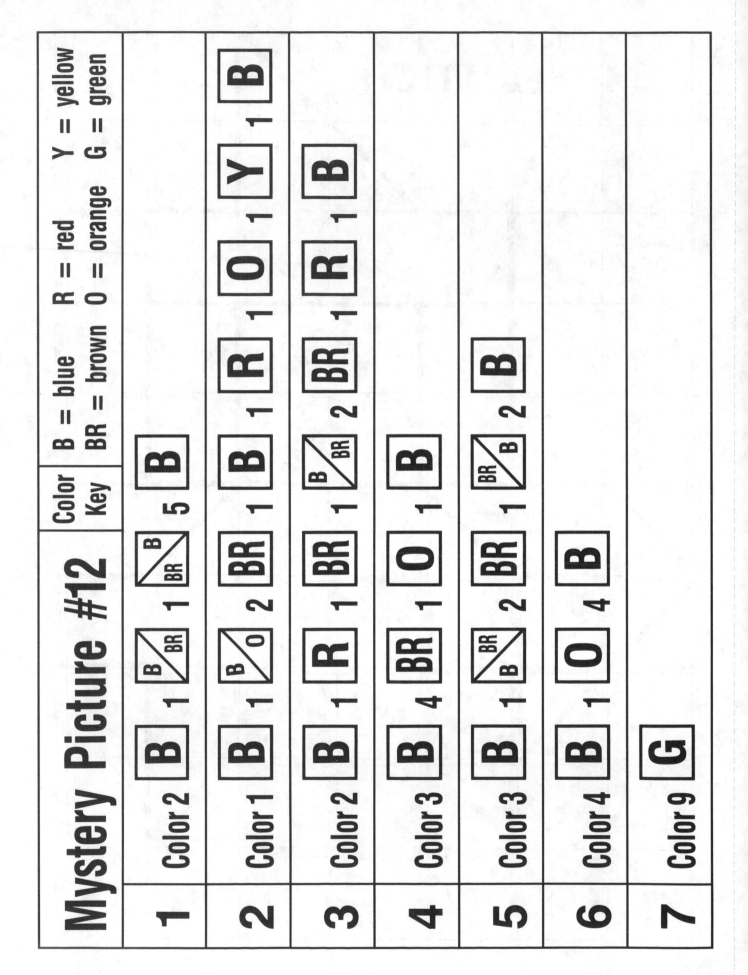

Color Key

B = blue	R = red	Y = yellow
BR = brown	O = orange	G = green

1	Color 2	B	1	B/BR	1	B/BR	5	B			
2	Color 1	B	1	B/O	2	BR	1	B	1	R	1	O	1	Y	1	B
3	Color 2	B	1	R	1	BR	1	B/BR	2	BR	1	R	1	B
4	Color 3	B	4	BR	1	O	1	B
5	Color 3	B	1	BR/B	2	BR	1	BR/B	2	B
6	Color 4	B	1	O	4	B
7	Color 9	G

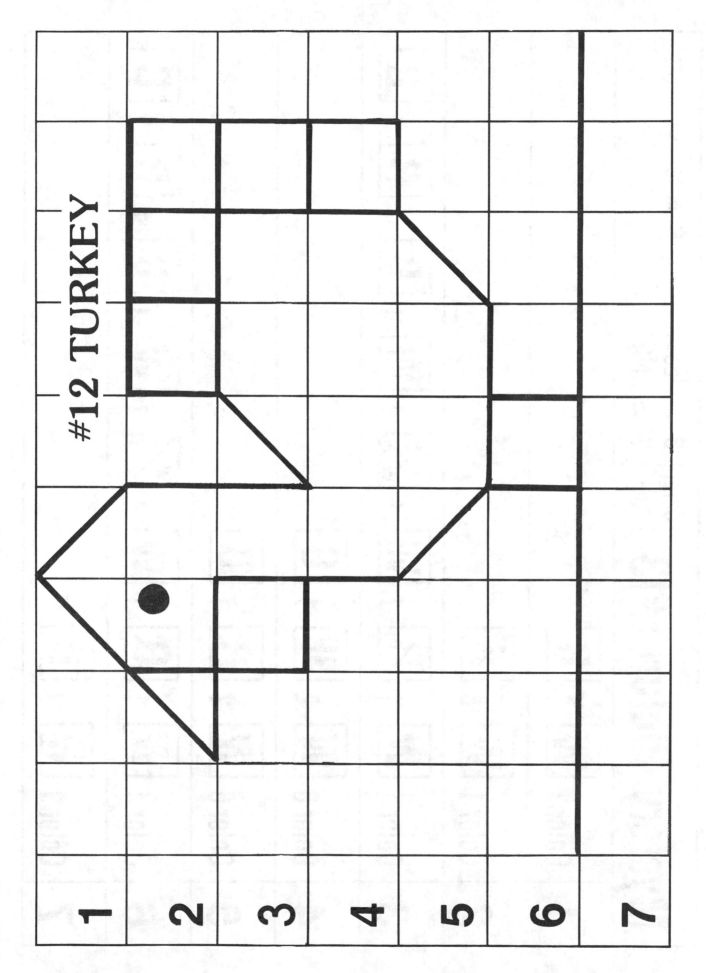

1 2 3 4 5 6 7

Mystery Picture #13

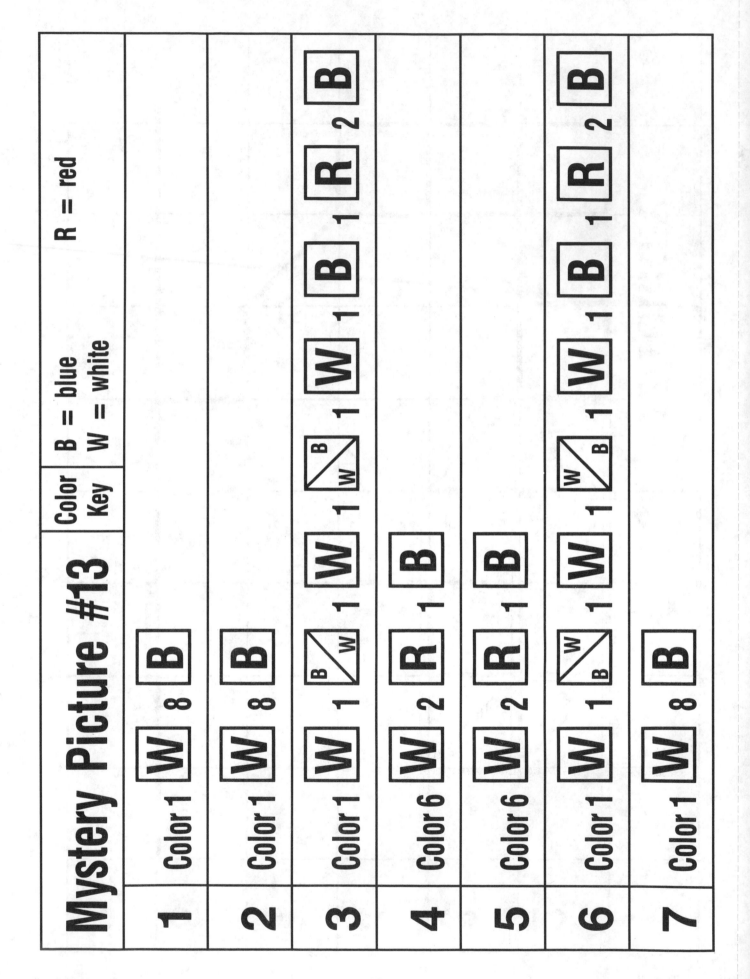

Color Key: B = blue W = white R = red

#13 SNOWMAN

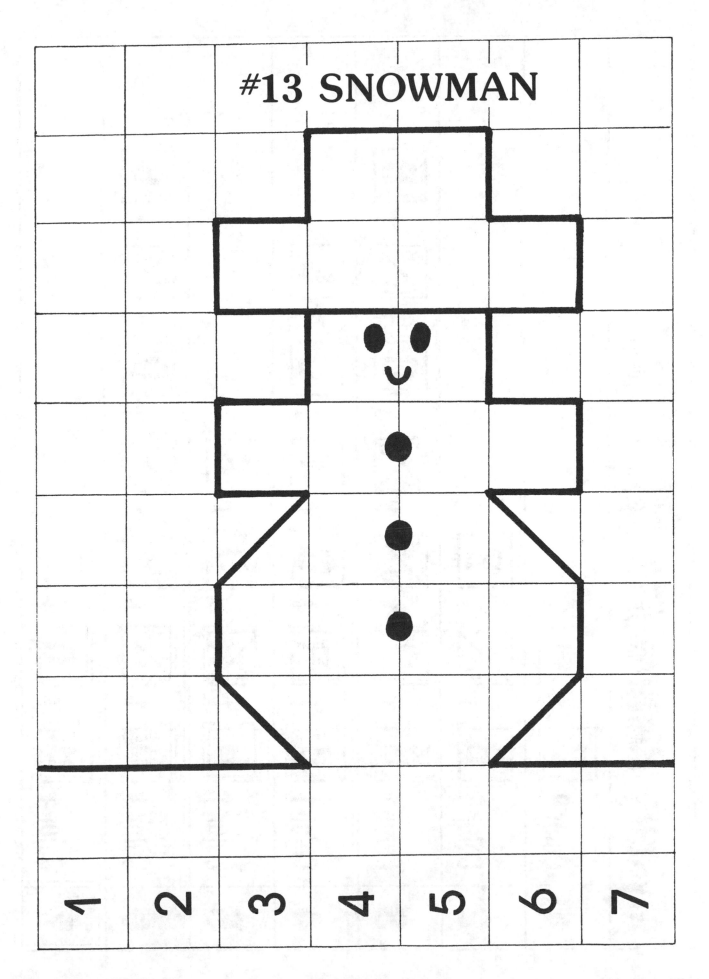

#095 Simple Graph Art

Mystery Picture #14

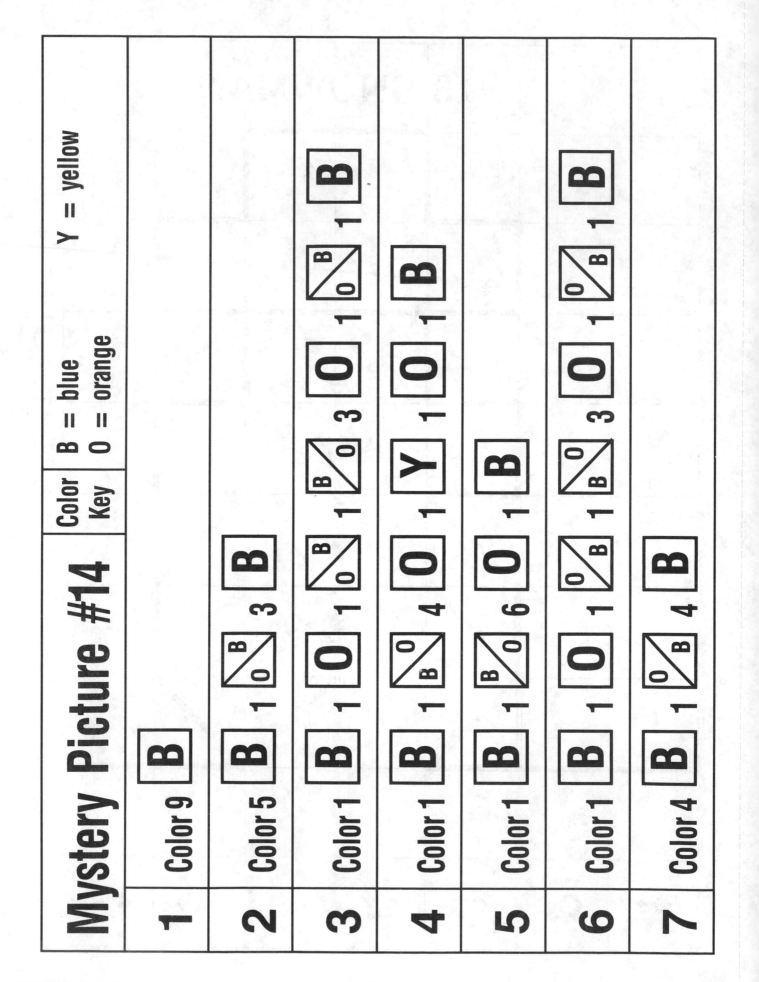

Color Key: B = blue O = orange Y = yellow

#14 FISH

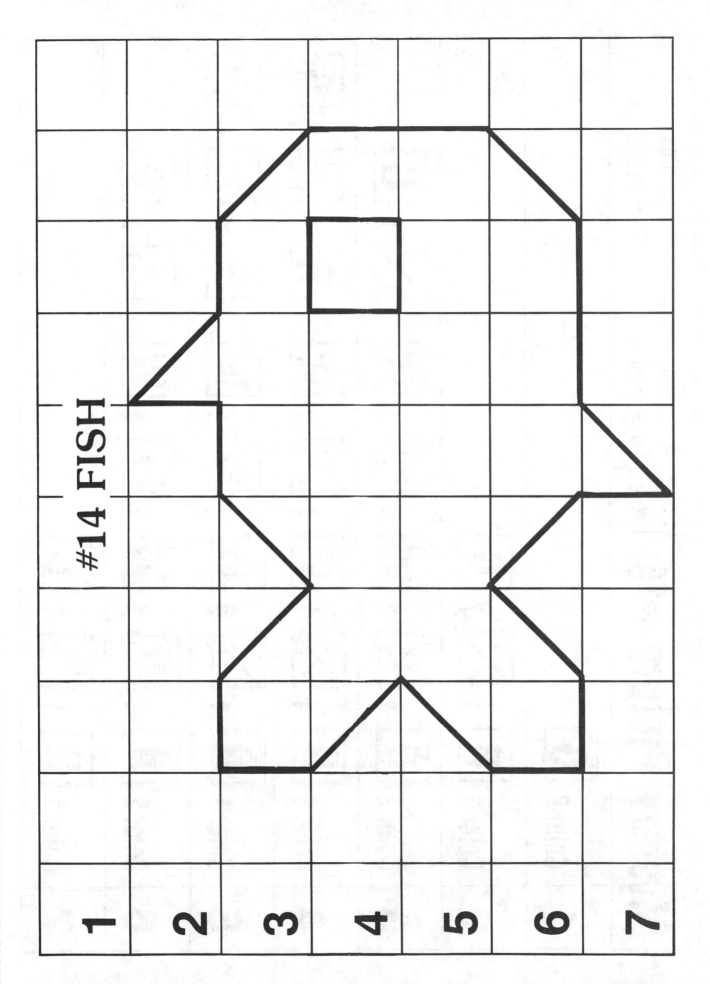

Mystery Picture #15

Color Key

R = red   PK = pink
W = white   G = green

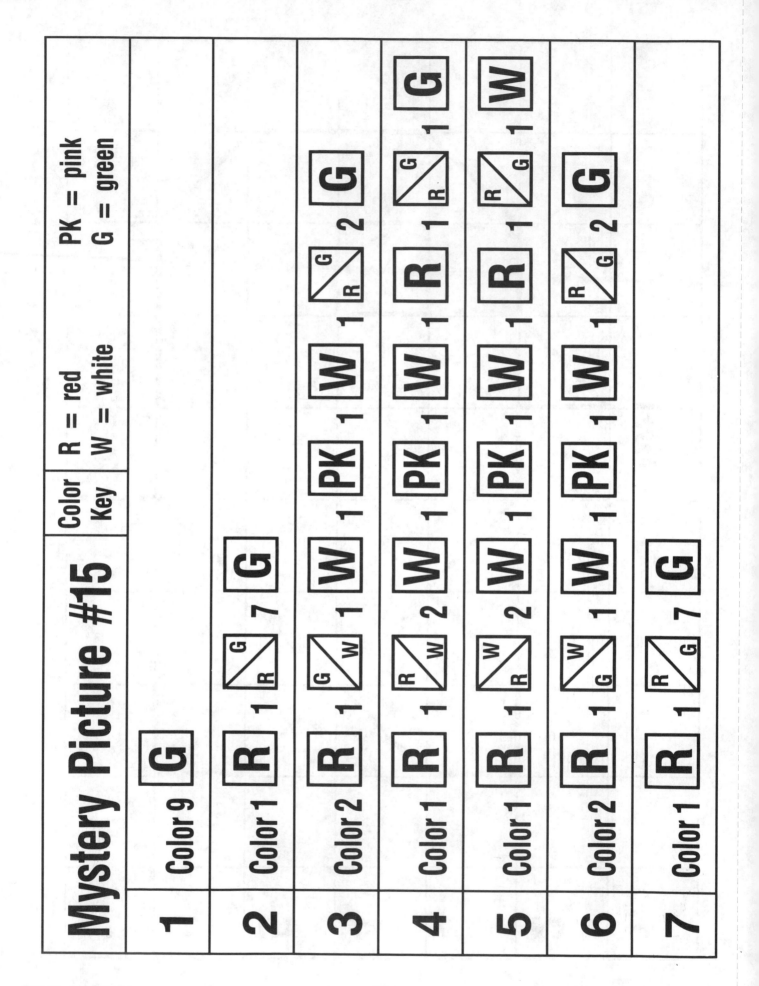

	Color						
1	9 G						
2	1 R	1 R/G	7 G				
3	2 R	1 G/W	1 PK	1 W	2 R/G	2 G	
4	1 R	1 R/W	1 PK	1 W	1 R/G	1 G	
5	1 R	1 W/R	1 PK	1 W	1 R/G	1 W	
6	2 R	1 W/G	1 PK	1 W	2 R/G	2 G	
7	1 R	1 R/G	7 G				

#15
SANTA CLAUS

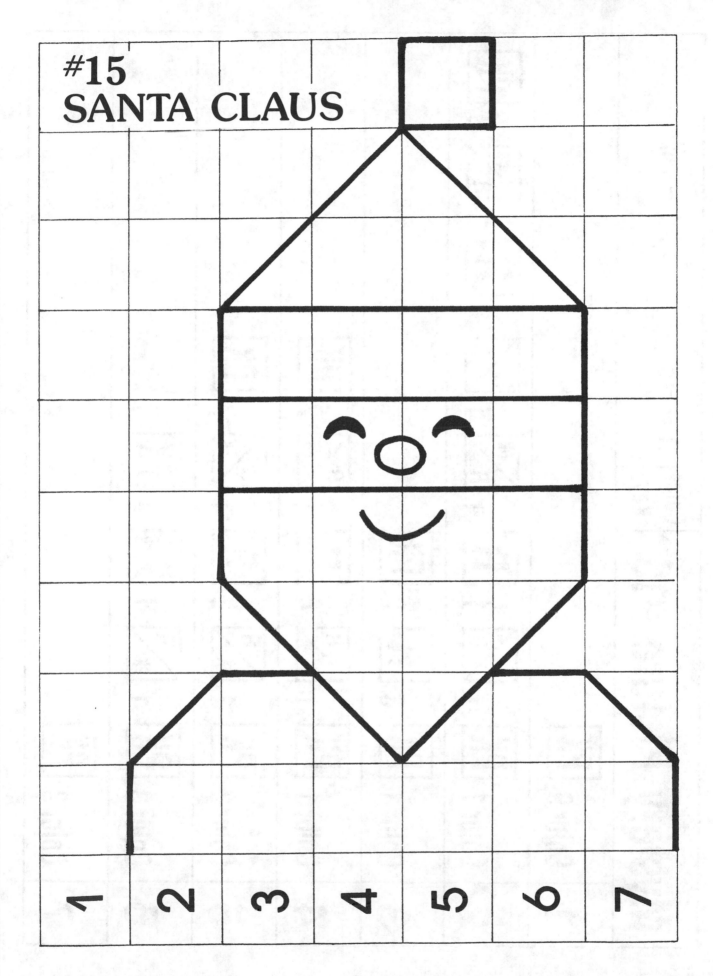

1 2 3 4 5 6 7

Mystery Picture #16

Color Key

R = red	PK = pink

1	Color 9 PK
2	Color 1 PK 1 PK/R 1 R 1 PK/R 1 R 1 PK/R 2 PK
3	Color 1 PK 6 R 2 PK
4	Color 1 PK 1 R/PK 4 R 1 R/PK 2 PK
5	Color 2 PK 1 R/PK 2 R 1 R/PK 3 PK
6	Color 3 PK 1 R/PK 4 PK
7	Color 9 PK

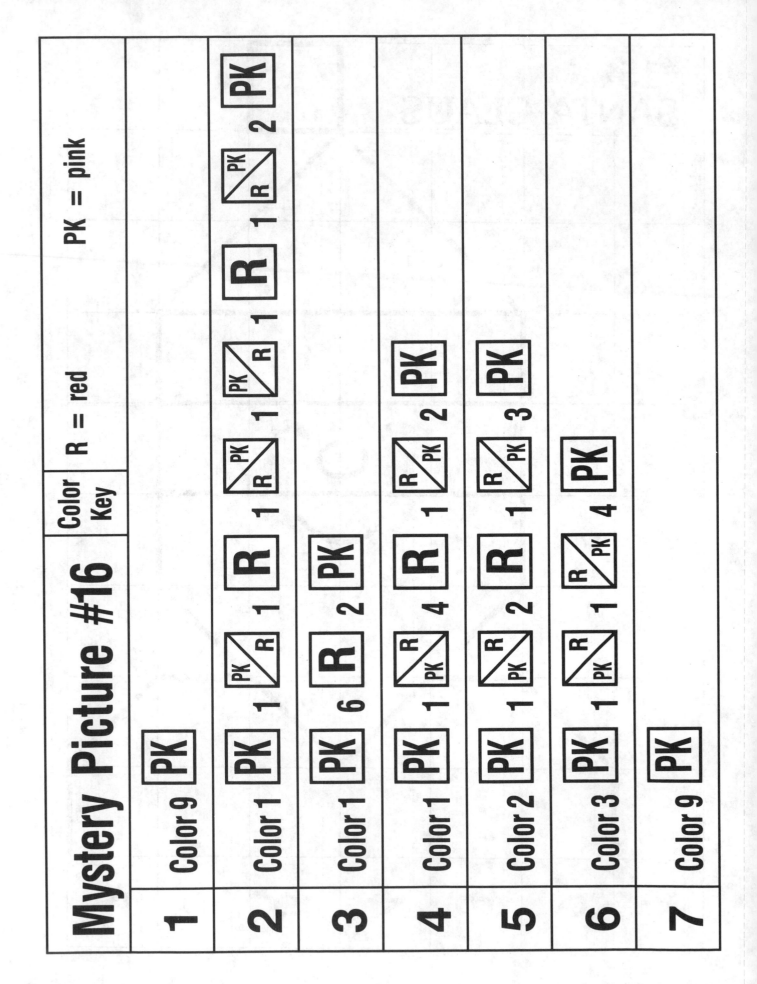

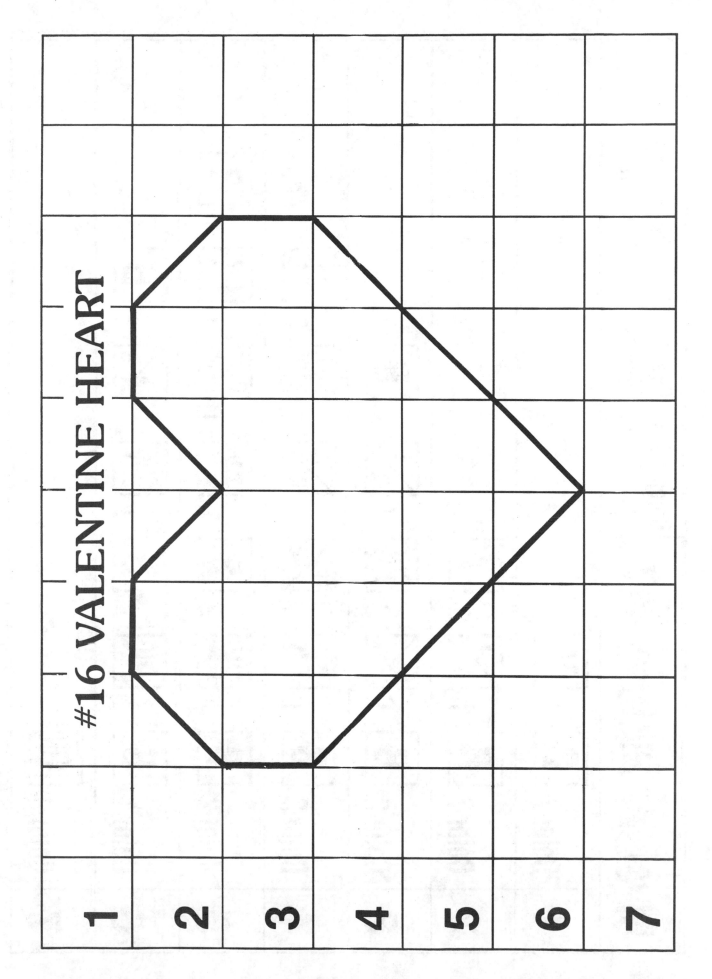

#16 VALENTINE HEART

1 2 3 4 5 6 7

Mystery Picture #17

Color Key	B = blue	PK = pink
	Y = yellow	G = green

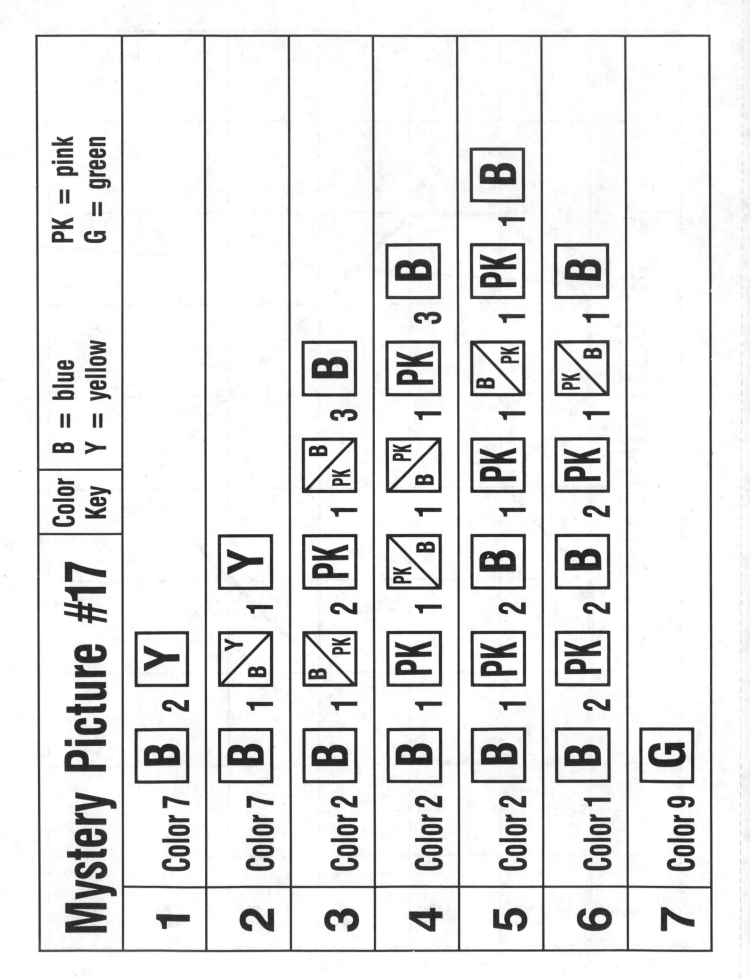

1	Color 7: B, Y 2
2	Color 7: B 1, B/Y 1
3	Color 2: B 1, B/PK 2, B/PK 1, B 3
4	Color 2: B 1, PK 1, PK/B 1, PK/PK 1, PK 3, B
5	Color 2: B 1, PK 2, B 1, PK 1, B/PK 1, PK 1, B
6	Color 1: B 2, PK 2, PK/B 1, B 1
7	Color 9: G

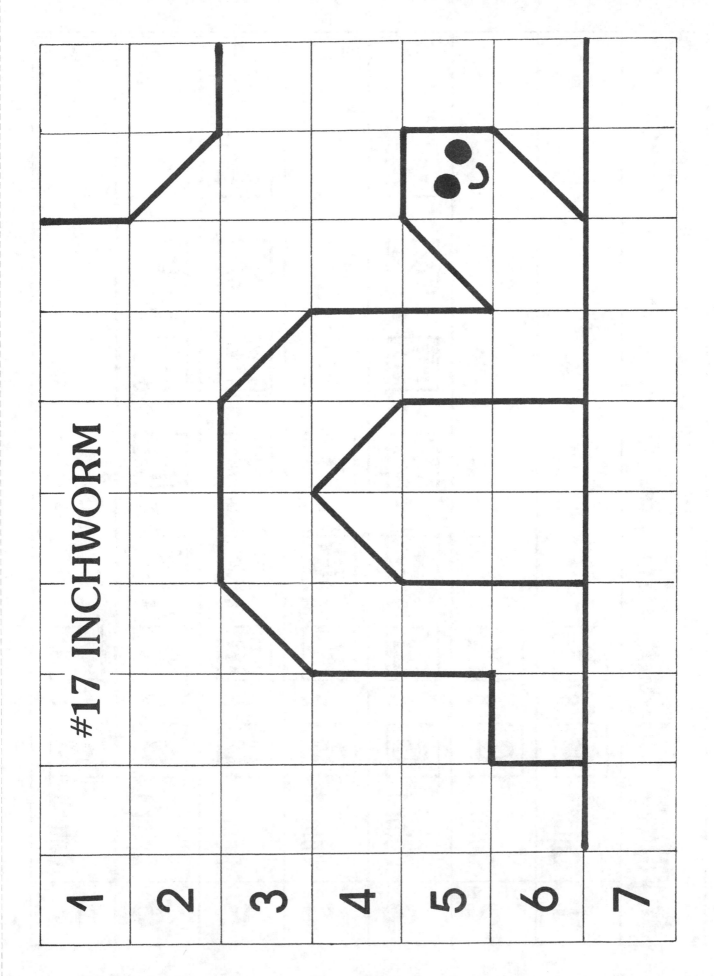

#17 INCHWORM

Mystery Picture #18

Color Key
GY = gray   G = green
Y = yellow

1	Color 1	G 8	Y
2	Color 1	G 8	Y
3	Color 1	G 3	GY 1 [Y/GY] 1 GY 1 [GY/Y] 1 Y
4	Color 1	G 2	Y 2 GY 4 Y
5	Color 1	G 3	GY 1 [GY/Y] 1 Y 1 GY 1 [Y/GY] 1 Y
6	Color 1	G 2	Y 1 GY 1 [GY/Y] 1 GY 3 [Y/GY]
7	Color 1	G 8	Y

#18 KITTEN

Mystery Picture #19

Color Key	
R = red	BK = black
GY = gray	G = green

	Instructions
1	Color 9 — R
2	Color 2 — R 1, R/GY 1, GY 4, R/GY 1, R 1
3	Color 2 — R 1, GY 1, BK 4, GY 1, R/GY 1
4	Color 1 — R 1, R/GY 6, GY 1, GY/R 1
5	Color 1 — R 1, GY/R 1, R/GY 1, R/GY 5, GY 1, R 1
6	Color 3 — R 2, GY 2, R 1, R 1
7	Color 9 — G

#095 Simple Graph Art

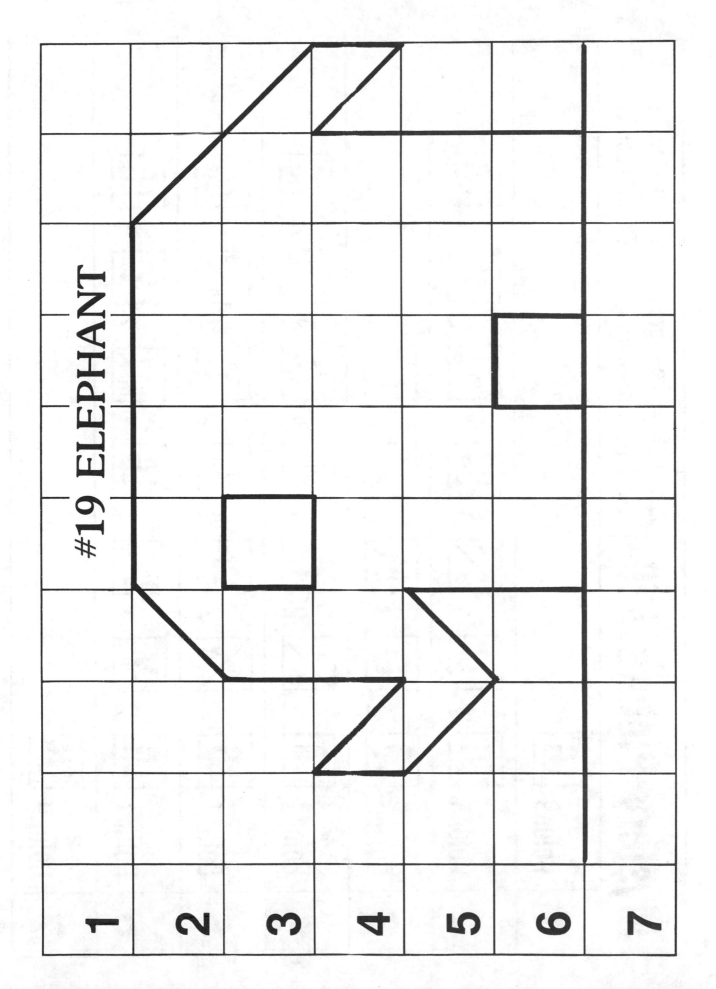

#19 ELEPHANT

41

Mystery Picture #20

Color Key: LG = light green Y = yellow O = orange BK = black

1 — Color 9 LG

2 — Color 1 LG 2 O 1 LG/O 1 BK 2 LG/O 1 O 1 LG

3 — Color 1 LG 3 O 1 BK 3 O 1 LG

4 — Color 1 LG 1 O/LG 2 O 1 BK 2 O 1 O/LG 1 LG

5 — Color 1 LG 1 LG/Y 2 Y 1 BK 2 Y 1 LG/Y 1 LG

6 — Color 1 LG 2 Y 1 Y/LG 1 LG 2 Y 1 Y/LG 1 LG

7 — Color 9 LG

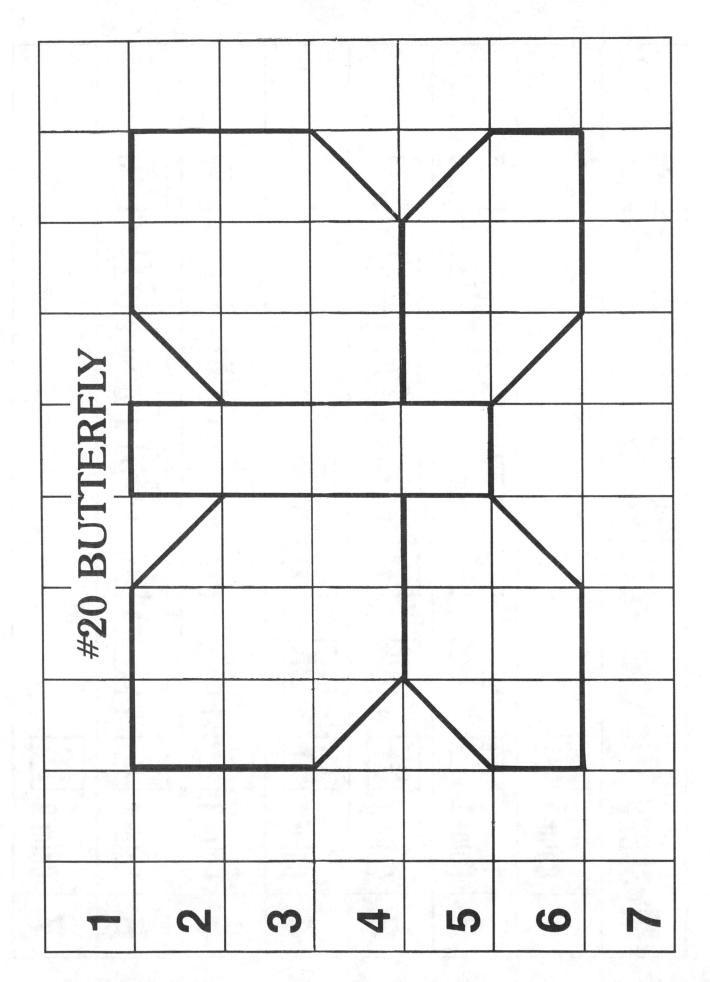

#20 BUTTERFLY

#095 Simple Graph Art

Mystery Picture #21

Color Key

LG = light green	BK = black
GY = gray	PK = pink

#	Instructions
1	Color 9 LG
2	Color 1 [LG\GY] 1 [GY] 2 [LG\GY] 1 [LG\GY] 1 [GY] 2 [LG\GY] 1
3	Color 3 GY 1 BK 1 [GY\PK] 1 PK 1 [PK\GY] 1 [GY\LG] 1
4	Color 2 GY 1 PK 2 LG 4
5	Color 3 GY 1 BK 1 [PK\GY] 1 PK 1 [PK\GY] 1 [LG\GY] 1
6	Color 1 [GY\LG] 1 GY 1 [GY\LG] 1 GY 2 [GY\LG] 1
7	Color 9 LG

#21 EASTER BUNNY

1 2 3 4 5 6 7

45

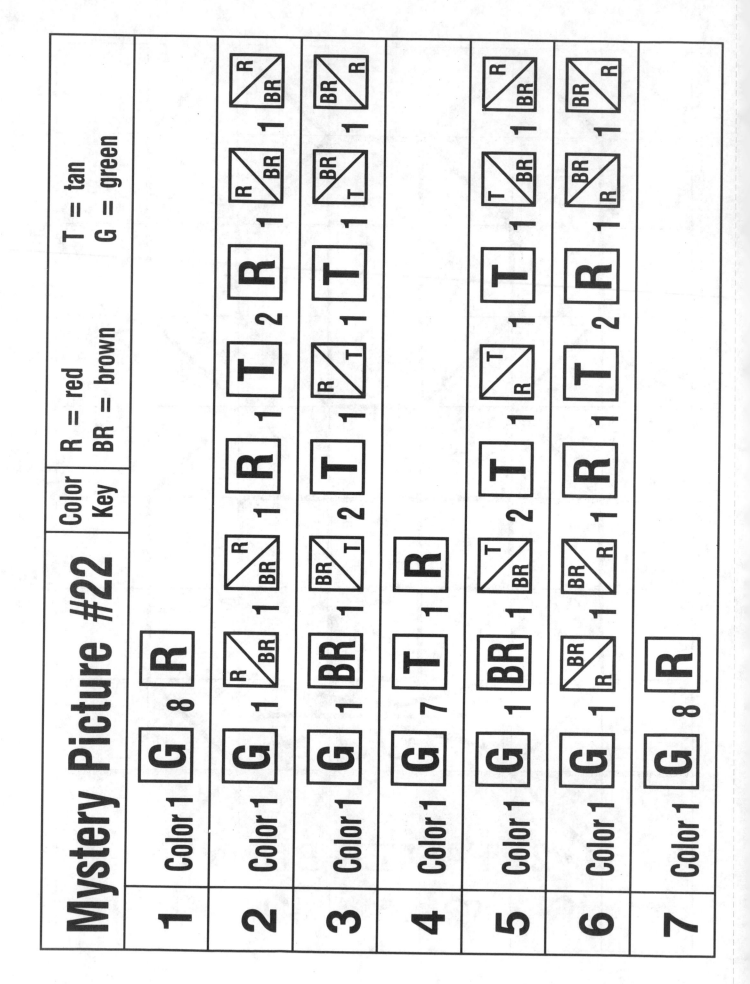

Mystery Picture #22

Color Key: R = red, BR = brown, T = tan, G = green

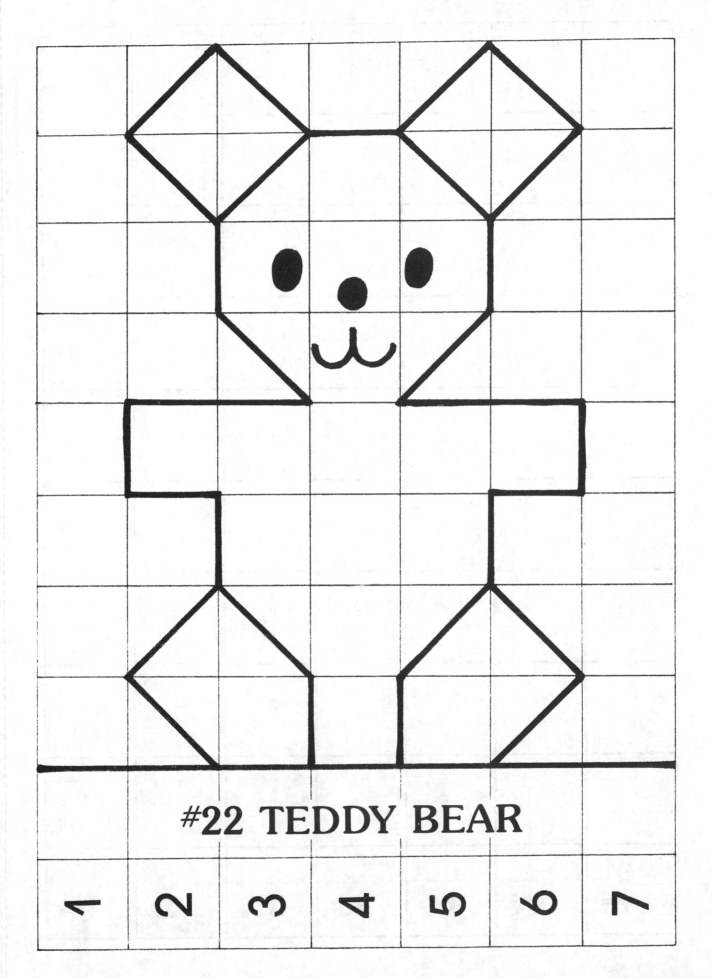

#22 TEDDY BEAR

1 2 3 4 5 6 7

1	2	3	4	5	6	7